⇢ 5-Minute ⇠
Prayer Journal
for Teen Girls

Daily Prompts for Guidance,
Praise, and Reflection

LOUISE HOLZHAUER

ROCKRIDGE
PRESS

Interior and Cover Designer: Irene Vandervoort
Art Producer: Megan Baggott
Editor: Elizabeth Baird
Production Editor: Ruth Sakata Corley
Production Manager: Holly Haydash

Illustrations ©Shutterstock
Author photo courtesy of Denise Habicht

Paperback ISBN: 978-1-63807-116-7
R0

To my husband, Greg, who has supported my writing in every possible way. I love you, and I am grateful. To my children, who may have taught me more than I taught them. To my granddaughters, Eva and Natalie; I am thinking of you. And to all the young women who take up a pen and pray: be blessed.

*Do not be anxious about anything,
but in every situation, by prayer
and petition, with thanksgiving,
present your requests to God.*

—Philippians 4:6

THIS BOOK BELONGS TO

....

→ Introduction ←

God already knows what's in your heart, so why pray? Why keep a prayer journal? As with most relationships, you'll grow closer to God if you sit down together and talk. What better way to find answers than by asking Him directly? God can help with everyday decisions. He can help you work through painful things. Nothing is off-limits, and He can't wait to hear from you! This little book offers a private place to pray and reflect on your own faith journey. There might even be some surprises for you along the way.

When I was 13 years old, I made some surprising discoveries about *my* life. My family moved to a larger city, and I suddenly began attending a huge, new school. While pretty scary at first, I got to experiment with the person I wanted to be by trying out all-new activities, relationships, and approaches to God. I found a great best friend, sang with a music group, and attended a Bible study for the first time. I still have the journal I used to record the struggles, the blessings, and the laughter I experienced. It reminds me that God has been watching over me my whole life.

As a counselor, I've learned many teens have a similar story, whether moving to a new place or facing other challenges. God designed teens to have a natural curiosity about life's biggest questions and about themselves. Writing down your thoughts makes room for that kind of exploration and opens the door to deeper understanding. Sharing your thoughts with God also allows Him to reveal your unique inner beauty. My prayer is that you will look back over this journal later and see how you've grown, what you've overcome, and the faithfulness of the One who loves you most of all.

How to Use
This Journal

This journal is designed to provide a simple yet powerful five-minute experience you can turn to daily—or whenever you choose. Each page begins with a Bible verse and a short explanation of the entry's theme. You'll then see two journaling prompts followed by two prayer prompts. I encourage you to write a few words or a few sentences for each one, sharing the thoughts of your heart with God. These daily journal entries are broken up by a day of praise every so often, to help you reflect on what you're feeling and learning.

If you can, sit by yourself in a quiet, comfortable place with your journal. Eliminate things that distract you. You are nurturing a relationship with the most important person in your life! Even if you set down this journal for a few days, I hope you come right back and start up where you left off. Feel free to really make it your own—write with colored pens or markers, doodle on the pages, and decorate them to match your moods. God will love it!

→ Hopes and Goals ←

Let's start your journaling adventure right now! Jot down some honest thoughts in the spaces provided below. (Remember, no one will read this but you.)

Writing out my prayers sounds ....

....

....

....

Some questions I have for God are ....

....

....

....

I'd like my relationship with Him to be more ....

....

....

....

When I'm finished with this journal, I hope ....

....

....

....

Your Journey

In their hearts humans plan their course,
but the Lord establishes their steps.
—Proverbs 16:9

When you write your prayers in this journal, you'll have both celebrations and disappointments to share. God understands all our experiences, and He can handle all our emotions. It's reassuring to know He's not only guiding us but walking right beside us on our journey.

I'm glad to know God was guiding my footsteps when __I discovered my goals and resolutions for the new year. He knows it is what I truly want to accomplish; he will guide me to success.__

Noticing God's presence in my life might help me __adapt into a peaceful life where I can share all of my feelings with a person I know I can trust.__

God, guide me in __productivity and love.__

Today, I pray for __my parents because of how much they have given me. I ask for them to be rewarded with peace.__

1

Salvation

For it is by grace you have been saved, through faith—
and this is not from yourselves, it is the gift of God.

—Ephesians 2:8

What have you done to earn your way into Heaven? That's a trick question. Heaven is a free gift for all who believe in Jesus. He takes the punishment for our sins and gives us His clean record. If you would like, you can ask God right now to forgive your sins and send His Holy Spirit to help you begin a new life with Him.

If someone asked me how to get to Heaven, I would tell them

....

....

....

I thank God for sending Jesus because ....

....

....

....

God, guide me in ....

....

....

Today, I pray for ....

....

....

Identity

*See what great love the Father has lavished on us,
that we should be called children of God!*

—1 John 3:1

Your most basic "Who am I?" identity is "child of God." As you explore
other things like personality traits, your likes and dislikes, and your
own gifts and talents, remember God meant to create *exactly you*.
In fact, you are the perfect instrument for the song God put in your
heart. So, go ahead and play it!

I'm glad God made me with the gifts/traits/abilities to ....

....

....

....

As a child of God, I want to ....

....

....

....

God, guide me in ....

....

....

Today, I pray for ....

....

....

Loneliness

If I rise on the wings of the dawn, if I settle on the far side of the sea, even there... your right hand will hold me fast.

—Psalm 139:9–10

Everyone feels lonely, more often than you know, sometimes even in a roomful of friends or a loving family. But God is always there to share your tears. Flesh-and-blood people meet our need for touch and laughter, but God is even nearer than flesh and blood. He is as close as your heart.

I sometimes feel lonely when ....

....

....

....

The next time I feel lonely, I could ....

....

....

....

God, guide me in ....

....

....

Today, I pray for ....

....

....

The Trinity

Therefore go and make disciples of all nations, baptizing them in the name of the Father and of the Son and of the Holy Spirit.
—Matthew 28:19

We use the word "Trinity" to describe the three persons of the God-head: Father, Son, and Holy Spirit. They exist like flames in a bonfire: seen individually, yet never really separate. And they are all acting in your life. The Father plans, the Son does His will, and the Spirit applies their work in our hearts.

I am grateful for the Father's plan to ....

....

....

....

I need the Holy Spirit for ....

....

....

....

God, guide me in ....

....

....

....

Today, I pray for ....

....

....

Hope

Why, my soul, are you downcast? Why so disturbed within me? Put your hope in God, for I will yet praise him, my Savior and my God.
—Psalm 42:11

Hope isn't always something you feel. Sometimes it's what you tell yourself, like "This is temporary. I can get through this." Sometimes it's in the form of a prayer request. When things seem dark, it's good to remember God always has a light waiting at the end of the tunnel. Remind yourself goodness is ahead. You can tell others, too.

I feel hope when ....

....

....

....

When I feel hopeless, I can tell myself ....

....

....

....

God, guide me in ....

....

....

....

Today, I pray for ....

....

....

....

Priorities

"Martha, Martha," the Lord answered, "you are worried and upset about many things, but few things are needed—or indeed only one."
—Luke 10:41–42

Jesus was letting Martha know that being with Him is more important than being the perfect hostess. Because we're all limited people, we have to choose what we'll be involved in and what we'll stand up for. That's not a bad thing. It makes us think about what's important to us—and whether those priorities line up with God's priorities.

My top three priorities are ....

....

....

....

Something I'd like to be a bigger priority is ....

....

....

....

God, guide me in ....

....

....

Today, I pray for ....

....

....

7

Heaven

[T]here before me was a throne in heaven with someone
sitting on it ... who had the appearance of jasper and ruby.
A rainbow that shone like an emerald encircled the throne.

—Revelation 4:2-3

Nobody knows exactly what Heaven will be like. The Bible talks about happiness, beauty, and seeing God face-to-face. Use your imagination to picture the things you hope to find there. Soaring mountains? Endless fudge cake? Whatever you imagine, it's sure to be even better!

I hope to find in Heaven ....

....

....

....

Seeing God for the first time will be ....

....

....

....

God, guide me in ....

....

....

Today, I pray for ....

....

....

God's Word

*I will instruct you and teach you in the way you should
go; I will counsel you with my loving eye on you.*

—Psalm 32:8

What if your favorite celebrity called or texted you every day with
practical advice for your life? Would you answer the phone, read that
advice? Well, the God of the universe, who loves you more than any
celebrity ever could, has already written to us about many things. All
we have to do is open His Word.

I could spend time in God's Word ....

....

....

....

God's Word to me means that He ....

....

....

....

God, guide me in ....

....

....

Today, I pray for ....

....

....

Being Yourself

*I will also give that person a white stone with a new name
written on it, known only to the one who receives it.*
—Revelation 2:17

We're going to get a new name in Heaven, perhaps our *real* name,
describing our true self. But you don't have to wait until then to start
being yourself. This is a great time of life to explore your talents and
temperament to find all the parts that feel true. Love all the good, true
things about yourself—God does!

If I could pick a new name for myself, I'd pick ....

....

....

A part of myself that feels true is ....

....

....

God, guide me in ....

....

....

Today, I pray for ....

....

....

Bullying

Learn to do right; seek justice. Defend the oppressed.
—Isaiah 1:17

During your teen years, there will probably be opportunities for you to defend someone who's being bullied at school or online. That might mean telling an adult, creating a distraction, confronting the bully, or comforting the person who's hurting. When you do, you'll be following the footsteps of Christ, who always cared for the suffering.

I saw bullying happen when ....

....

....

....

If I see someone being bullied, maybe I could ....

....

....

....

God, guide me in ....

....

....

Today, I pray for ....

....

....

Courage

Be strong and courageous. Do not be afraid or terrified because of them, for the Lord your God goes with you; he will never leave you nor forsake you.

—Deuteronomy 31:6

God stands with you, so don't let fear stop you from trying to achieve good things. Having courage doesn't mean we won't feel afraid. Courage is the strength to go forward when we *are* afraid. Maybe you won't succeed, but trust that great things will come from trying.

I was courageous when ....

....

....

....

I need God's strength to face ....

....

....

....

God, guide me in ....

....

....

....

Today, I pray for ....

....

....

....

Honesty

Do not steal. Do not lie. Do not deceive one another.
—Leviticus 19:11

Being honest doesn't mean you always have to tell your friend you hate her new haircut. What it *really* means is becoming a trustworthy person. Jesus called Himself "the Truth" because that's God's nature. If we cheat on a test or lie about breaking Mom's phone, we're moving away from God's heart. But when we practice honesty, we're becoming more like Him.

It's hard to be honest when ....

....

....

....

I'm glad I was honest when ....

....

....

....

God, guide me in ....

....

....

Today, I pray for ....

....

....

DATE: ___ / ___ / ___

Praise

"Praise" is complimenting God. You can admire His character (such as His wisdom, goodness, or love) or you can show appreciation for His work (like how He sent Jesus to die for us or something He's done in your own life). You can write, sing, say, or even sculpt your praises. There are lots of options! People like it when you compliment them, and so does God.

Flip back over your last few journal entries. Is there something you could use to praise God?

What is a compliment you most like to hear? How could you give that compliment to God?

Lord, I praise You for ....

....

....

....

....

....

....

....

....

New Life

Therefore, if anyone is in Christ, the new creation has come: The old has gone, the new is here!
—2 Corinthians 5:17

Our hearts melt when we see videos of newborn animals like puppies or ducklings. Life is such a miracle. Everything is brand-new. Everything is possible. When you have a personal relationship with Jesus as your Savior, that new creature is *you*. Every day, your life offers new possibilities.

If everything is possible, I hope ....

....

....

....

A part of my life I would like Jesus to renew is ....

....

....

....

God, guide me in ....

....

....

Today, I pray for ....

....

....

The Holy Spirit

*The Spirit himself testifies with our spirit
that we are God's children.*

—Romans 8:16

The Holy Spirit is God's gift of love. Everyone who sincerely asks Jesus into their life receives the Holy Spirit, who alerts us to sin, gives us the power to do good, and reminds us of God's Word. It's a gift that keeps on giving!

The Holy Spirit helps me ....

....

....

....

I am thankful for the Holy Spirit because ....

....

....

....

God, guide me in ....

....

....

....

Today, I pray for ....

....

....

....

Giving

Each of you should give what you have decided in
your heart to give, not reluctantly or under
compulsion, for God loves a cheerful giver.

—2 Corinthians 9:7

When your heart is full of God's love and goodness, it overflows in the act of giving. Your gift could be money, time, or a special skill. It might be in the form of volunteering at the church, donating winter coats to the homeless, or cheering up a friend in need. Whatever your offering may be, a gift from your heart makes God smile.

It felt really good when I gave ....

....

....

....

Something I'd like to give would be ....

....

....

God, guide me in ....

....

....

Today, I pray for ....

....

....

17

Body Image

*[T]he splendor of the heavenly bodies is one kind, and
the splendor of the earthly bodies is another.*
—1 Corinthians 15:40

Most of us can point out the flaws in our bodies, but we don't spend
much time thinking about the parts we like or the parts that
work well—until they stop working! God created our bodies in all
shapes, and gave them to us to care for. Our unique bodies are God's
amazing artwork.

A part of my body I like is ....

....

....

The human body is amazing because ....

....

....

God, guide me in ....

....

....

Today, I pray for ....

....

....

Working Together

So we rebuilt the wall till all of it reached half its height, for the people worked with all their heart.
—Nehemiah 4:6

Nehemiah tells the inspiring story of families rebuilding the wall around Jerusalem. The people worked together, carrying supplies, doing construction, and protecting other laborers. A giant project can be completed quickly when it's an enthusiastic group effort. Watch for opportunities God gives *you* to be part of such a team.

A group I saw work well together was ....

....

....

A group I might like to work with is ....

....

....

God, guide me in ....

....

....

Today, I pray for ....

....

....

19

Strong Emotions

As [Jesus] approached Jerusalem and
saw the city, he wept over it.
—Luke 19:41

Strong feelings can overwhelm us. Jesus wasn't embarrassed to show His emotions; we don't have to be, either. The trick is to *recognize* our emotions and take time with them. Thinking, journaling, talking to your bestie, and praying can help. Otherwise, your emotions might try to control you, instead of you controlling them.

My strongest emotions seem to appear ....

....

....

....

When I'm having trouble controlling my emotions, I could ....

....

....

....

God, guide me in ....

....

....

Today, I pray for ....

....

....

Online Presence

Don't let anyone look down on you because you are
young, but set an example for the believers in speech,
in conduct, in love, in faith and in purity.
—1 Timothy 4:12

We've all seen posts online that inspire us and those that make us uncomfortable. God has given you lots to say, so go ahead and say it. But, before you hit *Enter* ask yourself, "Am I setting an example I'd be proud for others to follow?"

My favorite things to post are ....

....

....

....

When people see me online, I want them to see ....

....

....

....

God, guide me in ....

....

....

Today, I pray for ....

....

....

Sisterhood

Where you go I will go, and where you stay I will stay.
Your people will be my people and your God my God.
—Ruth 1:16

Sometimes people think this Scripture verse is about marriage, but it's really about sisterhood. Ruth spoke these words to Naomi as they set off together for a new life full of unknowns and hardships. Being there for your sister and friend, and having her there for you, is one of the most amazing blessings God gives us.

I experience sisterhood with ....

....

....

Something I could do to strengthen my circle of sisters is ....

....

....

God, guide me in ....

....

....

Today, I pray for ....

....

....

Hard Work

To Adam he said, "Because you ... ate fruit from the
tree about which I commanded you ... through painful
toil you will eat food from [the ground]."
—Genesis 3:17

Sweat-drenched, achingly hard work only began when sin entered the world. Before that, all work was probably fun. But the effort has to be good for us because our loving Father prescribed it. When facing hard work, we can pray for strength, remembering God is also at work.

The hardest work I've ever done is ....

....

....

....

When I have hard work ahead, I want to ....

....

....

....

God, guide me in ....

....

....

Today, I pray for ....

....

....

Depression

In my distress I called to the Lord . . . and you listened to my cry.

—Jonah 2:2

We all have seasons of sadness, and that's okay. But depression is more than a bad day or a bad week. It's a sadness you can't climb out of, a dark cloud that colors everything gray for a long time. If you think you might be depressed, please tell someone who can help you. God will help you, too.

Right now, my world is the color of ....

....

....

....

If I became really depressed, I think I could tell ....

....

....

....

God, guide me in ....

....

....

Today, I pray for ....

....

....

Family

Anyone who does not provide for their relatives, and especially for their own household, has denied the faith.
—1 Timothy 5:8

A few people in the early Church were not taking care of their own close relatives. God puts a high priority on the family He gives us. We get to choose our friends, and to some extent our coworkers, teachers, and pastors, but God assigns us our family—to love and to care for.

I thank God for my family because ....

....

....

....

I could help take care of my family by ....

....

....

....

God, guide me in ....

....

....

Today, I pray for ....

....

....

Stewardship

*Now it is required that those who have been
given a trust must prove faithful.*
—1 Corinthians 4:2

God loans us some of His treasures. He gives us physical resources, like our possessions, our body, and the environment. He sends us relationships in our home, our church, and our neighborhood. God also gives us spiritual treasures like salvation, the Bible, and our personal gifts. God is pleased when we value these things the way He does.

Something I've been entrusted with is ....

....

....

....

One way I take care of God's treasures is ....

....

....

....

God, guide me in ....

....

....

Today, I pray for ....

....

....

Purpose

*So whether you eat or drink or whatever you
do, do it all for the glory of God.*
—1 Corinthians 10:31

Some people believe we each have one big purpose, like curing cancer
or saving gorillas. While God *might* want us to do those things, we
can actually accomplish His goal for us every day, in everything we
do. We don't have to stress over finding that one lifelong purpose. He's
already told us what it is. Just live for Him each day.

I think God was glorified when I ....

....

....

....

I could live for God today when ....

....

....

....

God, guide me in ....

....

....

Today, I pray for ....

....

....

DATE: ___ / ___ / ___

PRAISE AND REFLECT:
Simple Things

Sometimes it is the simple things that remind us of God. A butterfly in your yard lets you know He is there. An unexpected smile helps you feel His love. Waffles for breakfast make you think of His goodness. Be on the lookout today for small but beautiful things. They are all around you.

When God speaks through small things,
what could you say back to Him?

What are some small things that bring you joy?
Look back over your journal for ideas.

Is there anything around you right now
reminding you of God's presence?

Thank you, Lord, for sending me ....

....

....

....

....

....

....

....

Faith

Now faith is confidence in what we hope for and
assurance about what we do not see.

—**Hebrews 11:1**

Faith means trusting in something you can't completely prove. Most of us can't prove gravity will always be there or that tiny molecules exist, but we walk around believing in them. Relying on a God we can't totally prove to others is what sets Christians apart. If we could see or touch God, then we wouldn't *need* faith.

I believe in God because ....

....

....

....

The best thing about having faith in God is ....

....

....

....

God, guide me in ....

....

....

....

Today, I pray for ....

....

....

Responsibility

Whoever can be trusted with very little
can also be trusted with much.

—Luke 16:10

We all grow with our responsibilities. Generally, people start small, often with school and household chores. Being diligent and trustworthy in those situations shapes us for larger things later. Whether you find yourself wishing for more responsibility or less, what you do now is preparing you for future greatness!

A responsibility I have now is ....

....

....

....

Being trusted with responsibility makes me feel ....

....

....

God, guide me in ....

....

....

Today, I pray for ....

....

....

Confidence

*I care very little if I am judged by you or by any
human court; indeed, I do not even judge myself.*
—1 Corinthians 4:3

When the Apostle Paul said this, he had confidence despite being
criticized by both the legal system and his own friends. He wasn't
ashamed to be himself, no matter what others said. That kind of confidence doesn't come from loving yourself. It comes from knowing you
are dearly loved by God—no matter what.

I was able to stay confident when ....

....

....

....

An area where I wish I had more confidence is ....

....

....

....

God, guide me in ....

....

....

Today, I pray for ....

....

....

Food

[D]o not worry about your life, what you will eat
or drink; or about your body . . . Is not life more
than food, and the body more than clothes?
—Matthew 6:25

Many of us struggle to eat healthy food in the right amounts, but God doesn't want food to preoccupy us. If that should happen, you can ask a parent, teacher, or counselor for help. Obsessing about food leaves too little room for all the other beautiful things God gives us.

I am grateful for food like ....

....

....

I'd like to change my thinking about food by ....

....

....

God, guide me in ....

....

....

Today, I pray for ....

....

....

Community

All the believers were together and had everything in common.
—Acts 2:44

Often, in the Bible, the word "you" refers to a group of people, as when Jesus said, "I am with *you* always." Early Church believers intentionally lived their lives together, united in Christ. What would it look like for us to be more purposeful about this, too?

People need each other because ....

....

....

....

I could be more intentional about community by ....

....

....

....

God, guide me in ....

....

....

Today, I pray for ....

....

....

....

Fear

*"Do not be afraid of them, for I am with you and
will rescue you," declares the Lord.*
—Jeremiah 1:8

The Bible often tells us not to be afraid, but what does that mean?
Picture a small child frightened by a storm who runs into his mother's
arms. As she pats him gently, she whispers, "Don't be afraid, little
one. I've got you." When God tells us not to fear, He's reminding us
tenderly that He's got us.

Right now, I am feeling afraid of ....

....

....

I feel God's comfort when ....

....

....

God, guide me in ....

....

....

Today, I pray for ....

....

....

Making Friends

Therefore encourage one another and build each other up.
—1 Thessalonians 5:11

People often choose friends based on hobbies, like sports, or shared goals, like good grades. Sometimes we choose our friends based on appearance or popularity. But God advises us to look at the hearts of those around us. Kindness and goodness make the best friends.

I generally choose my friends based on ....

....

....

When I think about someone kind and good, I think of ....

....

....

God, guide me in ....

....

....

Today, I pray for ....

....

....

Waiting

Wait for the Lord; be strong and take
heart and wait for the Lord.

—Psalm 27:14

It's hard to wait—for your driver's license, for summer vacation, or for the end of the next commercial. But waiting is really important when big choices are involved. We make better decisions when we take time to let God work in us and our circumstances. When it's God we're waiting for, it's always worth it.

Right now I'm waiting for God to ....

....

....

I find it hard to wait when ....

....

....

God, guide me in ....

....

....

Today, I pray for ....

....

....

Tears

*As she stood behind him at his feet weeping, she
began to wet his feet with her tears.*
—Luke 7:38

Here we see a woman, forgiven and healed by Jesus, pouring the tears of her difficult life over his feet. She wept for a world that isn't always good and in gratitude for Jesus's love. We can give Him our tears, too. Our grief over sin or loss and our longing for God produce worthy tears of worship.

I think tears can be worship if ....

....

....

....

I worshiped God with my tears when ....

....

....

....

God, guide me in ....

....

....

Today, I pray for ....

....

....

Contentment

I have learned the secret of being content in any and every situation ... I can do all this through him who gives me strength.
—Philippians 4:12–13

Everyone longs for things they don't have: more money, a different body, stronger talents, or closer friends. It's hard to be content with unfulfilled wishes on your mind. So, Paul tells us his secret for being content in all circumstances: lean on God, who provides everything we need—even contentment.

The last time I felt content was ....

....

....

It's hard for me to be content when ....

....

....

God, guide me in ....

....

....

Today, I pray for ....

....

....

Respect

*Show proper respect to everyone, love the family
of believers, fear God, honor the emperor.*

—1 Peter 2:17

God asks us to respect everyone. God-given roles, like parent or
teacher or president, are to be respected, regardless of the person's
attitude or actions. Basic politeness, a calm demeanor, and using a
person's proper name are all simple ways of showing respect. We can
still challenge authority when necessary, but respectfully.

Thank you for people who are easy to respect, like ....

....

....

....

Lord, help me show more respect for ....

....

....

....

God, guide me in ....

....

....

Today, I pray for ....

....

....

Womanhood

Charm is deceptive, and beauty is fleeting; but a woman who fears the Lord is to be praised. Honor her for all that her hands have done, and let her works bring her praise.

—Proverbs 31:30–31

You are in the process of becoming the woman God dreamed about when He created you. Your dreams might involve a career or a relationship. Whatever you do, God dreams you will always put Him first, explore your gifts, and do wonderful things for *His* sake.

I think I am becoming a woman who ....

....

....

....

I dream someday I might ....

....

....

....

God, guide me in ....

....

....

....

Today, I pray for ....

....

....

Peer Pressure

Am I now trying to win the approval of human beings, or of God?
—Galatians 1:10

It's natural to want people to like us. But it can be risky, too. Our peers aren't always wise, and they don't always have our best interest at heart. When we're tempted to give in to peer pressure, we can check in with an older person we trust—and with God. He always has our best interest at heart.

I find myself trying to please my peers when ....

....

....

When I'm feeling pressured, I could ....

....

....

God, guide me in ....

....

....

Today, I pray for ....

....

....

41

PRAISE AND REFLECT:

Worship

Some people think worship is the same thing as church. But worship happens anytime we engage with God. When we bring Him our concerns, thank Him for His gifts, tell Him we're sorry, or celebrate something with Him, we are worshiping. In fact, everything in life is an opportunity for worship!

Are there times you have been worshiping without knowing it? Describe a few.

How does writing in your prayer journal seem like it might be worship?

Think about what you like best in worship at your church. Is there a way you could practice that element at home, too?

Lord, I worship You because ....

....

....

....

....

....

....

....

God's Mercy

But God demonstrates his own love for us in this:
While we were still sinners, Christ died for us.

—Romans 5:8

Mercy is bigger than just being nice to people. Think about someone who's hurt you. Would you put your own life on the line for them? Well, that's what Jesus did for us. We needed someone to pay the debt for our sins, and before we turned to Him, He had already died for us.

Describe how big God's mercy seems to you. ....

....

....

....

I need God's mercy because ....

....

....

....

God, guide me in ....

....

....

Today, I pray for ....

....

....

Anxiety

Therefore, do not worry about tomorrow, for tomorrow will worry about itself. Each day has enough trouble of its own.
—Matthew 6:34

God knows it helps to *limit* our anxious thoughts, like refusing to think about a problem that's days away or banning worries from the dinner table or your bedroom. A useful technique for reducing anxiety in the moment is to inhale slowly while saying to yourself, "The Lord is my shepherd"; then exhale slowly while saying, "I shall not want."

When I'm worried, it helps me to ....

....

....

....

Next time I'm worried, I'd like to try ....

....

....

....

God, guide me in ....

....

....

....

Today, I pray for ....

....

....

Your Light

In the same way, let your light shine before others, that they may see your good deeds and glorify your Father in heaven.
—Matthew 5:16

Can you see all the lanterns glowing in the darkness around you? There are selfless acts of courage, wisdom, goodness, and beauty everywhere. You have your own unique radiance, too. God gave you your own light to brighten the world. Shine it out! It's going to be amazing.

A patch of light I noticed recently was ....

....

....

I think I can shine for God by ....

....

....

God, guide me in ....

....

....

Today, I pray for ....

....

....

Strength

*But the Lord is faithful, and he will strengthen
you and protect you from the evil one.*
—2 Thessalonians 3:3

We need strength every day—for getting all our work done, helping others, resisting peer pressure, having patience, or bearing illness or pain. God promises to show up when we feel like we just can't do it. In fact, we probably shouldn't wait that long to ask Him for strength!

God recently gave me strength to ....

....

....

....

I'd like to ask for more strength to ....

....

....

....

God, guide me in ....

....

....

....

Today, I pray for ....

....

....

46

Being Left Out

A time is coming ... when you will be scattered ... You will leave me all alone. Yet I am not alone, for my Father is with me.

—John 16:32

Jesus predicted His friends would leave Him when things got hard, and they did. So Jesus understands us when we feel abandoned or left out; He went through it, too. But the same truth Jesus knew applies to us: we are never really alone. Never. God is always with us.

The times I feel most left out are ....

....

....

....

I could remind myself God is with me by ....

....

....

....

God, guide me in ....

....

....

....

Today, I pray for ....

....

....

Media

Do not conform to the pattern of this world, but be transformed by the renewing of your mind.

—Romans 12:2

It's not wrong to spend a little time relaxing with music, movies, or social media. But we need to be careful about what we're consuming and for how long. It's worth asking if our leisure choices bring peace and renewed energy or if they lead to sin, unhappiness, or addiction. The world doesn't always want what's best for us—but God does!

Most of my media time is ....

....

....

....

I might need to make some changes, such as ....

....

....

....

God, guide me in ....

....

....

....

Today, I pray for ....

....

....

Helping Others

God . . . will not forget your work and the love you have shown him as you have helped his people and continue to help them.
—Hebrews 6:10

When you take care of someone's pet or wash their car, you are being considerate and helpful. But do you realize you're also serving God? Whether you tutor a classmate, serve in a soup kitchen, or do laundry with your sister, helping others is a great way to show your love for the Lord.

I was glad when someone helped me ....

....

....

....

It felt good when I was able to help ....

....

....

....

God, guide me in ....

....

....

Today, I pray for ....

....

....

Siblings

And he has given us this command: Anyone who loves
God must also love their brother and sister.
—1 John 4:21

This Scripture asks us to love those closest to us—our siblings. But they can sometimes be the hardest people to love. Think about how you treat visitors in your home versus your brother or sister. Next time you're feeling testy with a sibling, maybe you could try treating them like a guest instead of a family member!

My sibling(s) and I treat each other ....

....

....

....

If my sibling(s) were a stranger, I would treat them ....

....

....

....

God, guide me in ....

....

....

Today, I pray for ....

....

....

Dating

*Be devoted to one another in love. Honor
one another above yourselves.*
—Romans 12:10

The Bible doesn't have much to say about dating, mostly because
people back then didn't date like we do now. However, the Bible has
a lot to say about treating each other with honor and holy love. It's
important to treat your date with respect and kindness and to expect
the same treatment in return.

My treating a date with honor would look like ....

....

....

....

A date treating me with honor would look like ....

....

....

....

God, guide me in ....

....

....

Today, I pray for ....

....

....

Struggles

*I have fought the good fight, I have finished
the race, I have kept the faith.*

—2 Timothy 4:7

Everyone has problems. It's part of being human. Jesus wept. The
disciples were confused. And here is Paul describing his life as a fight!
It's an impossible goal to live without struggles. The real goal, as Paul
understood it, is to *struggle well*. God won't remove all our battles, but
He will fight them with us.

I think I struggled well with ....

....

....

....

A struggle I could use God's help with is ....

....

....

....

God, guide me in ....

....

....

Today, I pray for ....

....

....

Music

[A]t his sacred tent I will sacrifice with shouts of joy; I will sing and make music to the Lord.

—Psalm 27:6

Did you know all the psalms are actually song lyrics written for worship? Music inspires our feelings and helps us express them. When you need an emotional lift, or feel like being loud, music can do that. When you want to worship God, the right music can do that, too.

I enjoy music when ....

....

....

....

Music helps me worship by ....

....

....

God, guide me in ....

....

....

Today, I pray for ....

....

....

Death

And whoever lives by believing in me will never die.
—John 11:26

Almost everyone is afraid of death. But, if we have faith in Jesus Christ, we don't need to be afraid. Our spirits have already been given eternal life! Our bodies will die at some point, but our souls never will. We will join the community of Heaven to live with God in love and delight.

I sometimes feel afraid of death because ....

....

....

....

Knowing my spirit will never die helps me ....

....

....

....

God, guide me in ....

....

....

....

Today, I pray for ....

....

....

Kindness

Therefore, as God's chosen people, holy and dearly loved, clothe yourselves with compassion, kindness, humility, gentleness and patience.
—Colossians 3:12

Kindness is like a favorite sweater. It makes us feel warm, calm, and safe. Kind people show they care by treating others gently and giving them the benefit of the doubt. We can extend that same warmth to others by putting on kindness, with God's help.

I'm glad I was kind when ....

....

....

....

A kind person in my life is ....

....

....

....

God, guide me in ....

....

....

Today, I pray for ....

....

....

PRAISE AND REFLECT:

Peace

It's hard to find peace in the modern world, to set aside our busyness and distractions. Jesus knew it would be hard for the disciples, too. One of the last things He said to them was "Peace I leave with you; my peace I give you. I do not give to you as the world gives. Do not let your hearts be troubled and do not be afraid."—John 14:27

Looking back over your recent journal entries, are there areas where you need to find God's peace?

Can you think of calming places you can retreat to when you need God's peace?

Try sitting quietly and reading John 14:27 a few times. Can you feel God's peace? What are ways you can carry that peace throughout the day or during difficult times?

Thank you, Lord, for offering me Your peace when ....

....

....

....

....

....

....

....

....

Sinners

[F]or all have sinned and fall short of the glory of God.
—Romans 3:23

Everybody we will ever meet is a sinner, including your grandma, your best friend, and your pastor. We won't completely outgrow our sinfulness as long as we live. It helps to know this so we can be on the lookout for sin in ourselves, and so we can show compassion for other sinners.

An area of sin in my own heart might be ....

....

....

Help me have compassion for other sinners when ....

....

....

God, guide me in ....

....

....

Today, I pray for ....

....

....

God's Forgiveness

*For I will forgive their wickedness and will
remember their sins no more.*

—Hebrews 8:12

When someone hurts or betrays us, the relationship suffers. That's exactly what happens in our relationship with God when we sin. It hurts God's heart, and we need a bridge to get us back to Him. So, God built a bridge called forgiveness, and He's ready to extend that bridge every time we need it.

I need forgiveness for ....

....

....

....

God's forgiveness means I can ....

....

....

....

God, guide me in ....

....

....

....

Today, I pray for ....

....

....

....

Self-Control

Like a city whose walls are broken through
is a person who lacks self-control.

—Proverbs 25:28

Controlling our mouths, our actions, and our choices is challenging, even for adults. Some ways we can help ourselves include noticing when we're out of control, practicing self-calming techniques like deep breathing and prayer, and being accountable to trusted friends. Self-control pleases God *and* protects us.

I would like more self-control in ....

....

....

....

Something I could do to help my self-control is ....

....

....

....

God, guide me in ....

....

....

Today, I pray for ....

....

....

Sleep

In peace I will lie down and sleep, for you
alone, Lord, make me dwell in safety.
—Psalm 4:8

Sleep is a kind of barometer. Too much sleep might indicate depression or illness. Too little sleep might mean you're experiencing anxiety or overwork. We all need a good night's sleep, and one way to get it is to remind yourself, as you lie down, that God will handle everything until morning.

I get too much or too little sleep because ....

....

....

....

I would like to help myself with sleep by ....

....

....

....

God, guide me in ....

....

....

Today, I pray for ....

....

....

Self-Esteem

*You have made [people] a little lower than the angels
and crowned them with glory and honor.*

—Psalm 8:5

Feeling unimportant? Why, you're practically heavenly—God made you just a little lower than the angels! You have more dignity and value than you realize. God created you with extraordinary worth, and the Holy Spirit lives within you. If you're that special to God, it's important you value yourself, too. Crown yourself with some glory, girl!

I know I am valuable because ....

....

....

Really valuing myself would mean ....

....

....

....

God, guide me in ....

....

....

Today, I pray for ....

....

....

School

By wisdom a house is built, and through understanding
it is established; through knowledge its rooms are
filled with rare and beautiful treasures.
—Proverbs 24:3–4

Going to school is like lifting weights for your brain. It's hard, but it produces great results. God wants us to learn as much as possible so we can become everything He created us to be. And maybe we'll find some of those "rare and beautiful treasures" along the way.

I like to learn about

I need God's help to study because

God, guide me in

Today, I pray for

Humility

Do nothing out of selfish ambition or vain conceit.
Rather, in humility value others above yourselves.
—Philippians 2:3

Pride is human, but proud people don't share their hearts easily. A humble person can admit they might be wrong or need help. A humble person lets you see their mistakes, not just their successes. And a humble person makes others feel valued. While it's a risk to be that vulnerable, it's also how we connect with other people and with God.

A humble heart toward people would mean ....

....

....

....

A humble heart toward God would mean ....

....

....

....

God, guide me in ....

....

....

Today, I pray for ....

....

....

Compromise

It is better not to . . . do anything . . . that will
cause your brother or sister to fall.

—Romans 14:21

We can't compromise when it comes to some things, like our belief in Jesus's resurrection. But in things that don't really matter, compromise is a Biblical way to love the people around us. The next time you find yourself arguing over a pizza topping, a TV show, or a chore, ask yourself, "Is this really important?" If not, look for a compromise.

I made a compromise when ....

....

....

Something I wouldn't want to compromise is ....

....

....

God, guide me in ....

....

....

Today, I pray for ....

....

....

Happiness

*You who are young, be happy while you are young, and
let your heart give you joy in the days of your youth.*
—Ecclesiastes 11:9

Happiness is related to our circumstances. Anything from a hot fudge
sundae to a love note to a great nap can make us feel happy. When life
is good, God wants us to enjoy it with gratitude. Happiness is a gift!
We can share that special gift with others by making them happy, too.

I feel really happy when ....

....

....

....

I could give the gift of happiness to someone else by ....

....

....

....

God, guide me in ....

....

....

Today, I pray for ....

....

....

Bad Company

Do not make friends with a hot-tempered person, do not associate with one easily angered, or you may learn their ways and get yourself ensnared.

—Proverbs 22:24–25

As you explore new friendships during your teen years, God's Word advises you to pick friends you admire, who will help you be your best self. We tend to grow more like our friends, even if they're bad company. Surrounding ourselves with good people makes us better people!

In general, I want my friends to be ....

....

....

....

I would like to be more like my friend ....

....

....

....

God, guide me in ....

....

....

....

Today, I pray for ....

....

....

Attitude

*In your relationships with one another, have
the same mindset as Christ Jesus.*
—Philippians 2:5

Our attitude affects everyone around us. Christ had an attitude of
patience, humility, and kindness because He always let His Father fill
His heart. When you're feeling irritable or unhappy, as we all do occa-
sionally, try stepping away for some time with God. When your heart
is full of gratitude and grace, everyone will know it.

My attitude right now is ....

....

....

When I need a change of attitude, I could ....

....

....

God, guide me in ....

....

....

Today, I pray for ....

....

....

Healing

But He said to me, "My grace is sufficient for you, for my power is made perfect in weakness."

—2 Corinthians 12:9

When the Apostle Paul asked God for healing, God said no because Paul's ministry would be more amazing *with* his disability. When we need physical or emotional healing, we can turn to God in prayer like Paul did, knowing God will hear us and do whatever is best. God still heals. And sometimes, He still says no.

I saw God's healing at work when ....

....

....

....

I would like to be healed in the area of ....

....

....

....

God, guide me in ....

....

....

Today, I pray for ....

....

....

Mystery

"For my thoughts are not your thoughts, neither are your ways my ways," declares the Lord.

—Isaiah 55:8

Although we have the entire Bible to help us, God can still be pretty mysterious. How can He hear everybody's prayers at the same time? Why does He allow bad things to happen? When we get stumped by a mystery, we can rely on what we *do* know: God is in control; He loves us; He will work it all out in the end.

A mystery I wonder about is ....

....

....

....

When I think about mysterious things, I feel ....

....

....

....

God, guide me in ....

....

....

....

Today, I pray for ....

....

....

PRAISE AND REFLECT:
Prayer

The Lord's Prayer is one model for us (see Matthew 6:9–13), but there are many ways to pray. Prayer is a conversation. The important things are expressing yourself to God and making room to hear Him. You can pray before a meal, in the middle of a test, or during a fight with your BFF. God is *always* available.

What's one thing that has changed about your prayers since starting this journal?

Is there a time or a need during your day when you'd like to remember to pray?

Lord, I am glad for the privilege of prayer because ....

....

....

....

....

....

....

....

....

....

....

Guilt

If we confess our sins, he is faithful and just and will forgive us our sins and purify us from all unrighteousness.

—1 John 1:9

Guilt is the burden we carry around after we've done something wrong. God says there's an easy way to throw down that weight: just confess it to Him. He forgives us every time. Sometimes, it's harder to forgive ourselves. But if God can forgive us, we can too.

When I've done something wrong, I tend to ....

....

....

....

It helps me forgive myself when ....

....

....

....

God, guide me in ....

....

....

Today, I pray for ....

....

....

....

God's Love

Your love, Lord, reaches to the heavens,
your faithfulness to the skies.
—Psalm 36:5

There is no way we can measure God's great love for us. Sometimes we may feel distant from Him, but it's not because His love has gone away. It can help to look toward the sky and remember that all the space between God and us is filled with His love. It's always there, wrapping us in a warm hug.

I need to be reminded of God's love when ....

....

....

I'm glad God's love is bigger than ....

....

....

God, guide me in ....

....

....

Today, I pray for ....

....

....

Trust

*Some trust in chariots and some in horses, but
we trust in the name of the Lord our God.*

—Psalm 20:7

You probably don't trust in chariots very often! But we all have things
we do trust to help us, things like money or talent or friends. Those
aren't necessarily bad, but they'll fail us eventually. It's nothing personal. It's simply part of being human. Nothing and no one is perfect
except God; we need to make sure we trust Him most of all.

When I need help, I sometimes rely on ....

....

....

Right now, I will try to trust God for ....

....

....

God, guide me in ....

....

....

Today, I pray for ....

....

....

Pride

*If anyone thinks they are something when
they are not, they deceive themselves.*

—Galatians 6:3

If there's something we can do better than others, it's easy to feel *we* are better. Then again, when someone else is prettier, has more talent, or gets better grades than we do, it's easy to feel less-than. When we measure the people around us, we are also measuring ourselves. Pride is a liar, whether it tells us we are one up or one down.

I sometimes think I am less-than when ....

....

....

....

An area of pride I struggle with is ....

....

....

....

God, guide me in ....

....

....

Today, I pray for ....

....

....

Your Neighbor

"Which of these three do you think was a neighbor to the man [who was hurt]?" The expert in the law replied, "The one who had mercy on him."

—Luke 10:36–37

In the famous story of *the Good Samaritan,* Jesus explains our "neighbor" can be anyone at all: a family member, a stranger, or even an enemy. Showing mercy is obeying God's command to love your neighbor. Is there someone in your life who needs a good neighbor?

When Jesus tells us to love our neighbor, He means ....

....

....

....

A "neighbor" I've helped recently is ....

....

....

....

God, guide me in ....

....

....

....

Today, I pray for ....

....

....

Unity

*Make every effort to keep the unity of the
Spirit through the bond of peace.*
—Ephesians 4:3

Jesus told His disciples the world would see God's love through their unity. Unity doesn't mean Christians always agree. We have different thoughts about everything from fun activities to our ideas about God, but we can always try to listen, love, and respect each other.

I feel a sense of unity when ....

....

....

....

Unity in the Church is ....

....

....

God, guide me in ....

....

....

Today, I pray for ....

....

....

Grief

He will wipe every tear from their eyes. There will be
no more death or mourning or crying or pain.

—Revelation 21:4

We might grieve a pet's death, a divorce in the family, the end of a friendship, or a lost possession. The deepest grief of all is losing a loved one. But, we can talk to God about our pain, knowing He understands. He will sit with us and catch our tears, sharing His promise that it won't be this way forever.

The deepest grief I've experienced is ....

....

....

....

God comforts me in the sadness of grief by ....

....

....

....

God, guide me in ....

....

....

Today, I pray for ....

....

....

Making Connections

The foreigner residing among you must be treated
as your native-born. Love them as yourself,
for you were foreigners in Egypt.
—Leviticus 19:34

God asks us to treat people who are different from us with love. It can start with a connection. Talking to the new girl at lunch or the visitor who doesn't speak a lot of English can feel scary. But it's an act of love God would be proud of. And you just might get a new friend out of it.

I made a connection with someone different when ....

....

....

....

Someone reached out to me when ....

....

....

....

God, guide me in ....

....

....

....

Today, I pray for ....

....

....

....

Perseverance

Therefore . . . let us throw off everything that hinders and the sin that so easily entangles. And let us run with perseverance the race marked out for us.

—Hebrews 12:1

Distractions, bad habits, and temporary problems can stop us for a moment, but God urges us on. Your life has been given to you for God's own secret and special purposes. You don't have to know exactly what those are; you just have to keep going!

Maybe I should throw off ....

....

....

....

I need God's help to persevere in ....

....

....

....

God, guide me in ....

....

....

....

Today, I pray for ....

....

....

Favoritism

*Do not pervert justice; do not show partiality to the poor or
favoritism to the great, but judge your neighbor fairly.*
—Leviticus 19:15

Everybody has felt the pain of not being the favorite niece or
student or athlete. Being treated unfairly hurts. It makes us angry.
Here on earth, justice will never be perfect, but when we meet God
face-to-face, all those wrongs will be made right. God asks us to try to
be fair with other people, because He is going to be fair with all of us.

An example of unfair treatment I've felt is ....

....

....

....

I really tried to be impartial when ....

....

....

....

God, guide me in ....

....

....

Today, I pray for ....

....

....

Control

And we know that in all things God works for the good of those who love him, who have been called according to his purpose.

—Romans 8:28

Some people like to be in control, but others find it a scary responsibility. It's comforting to remember God stands behind it all, invisibly, guiding things toward His purposes. It's great to know even our mistakes (or other people's) can't overrule God's plans for us.

Having control of something makes me feel ....

....

....

....

When things feel out of control, I can try to remember ....

....

....

....

God, guide me in ....

....

....

Today, I pray for ....

....

....

81

Remembering

Remember the wonders he has done, his miracles,
and the judgments he pronounced.
—1 Chronicles 16:12

It's not just old people who forget things. We all pay a lot more attention to today than yesterday. It's nice to spend some time remembering what God's done for us. Journaling is a good way to help us remember all the joys, the lessons, and the people He's given us.

Looking back through this journal, one thing I want to remember is ....

....

....

....

Remembering can be hard because ....

....

....

....

God, guide me in ....

....

....

Today, I pray for ....

....

....

Hospitality

Do not forget to show hospitality to strangers, for by so doing some people have shown hospitality to angels without knowing it.

—Hebrews 13:2

Hospitality means making others feel welcome, whoever they are, and wherever you are. Hosting an international student, organizing a sleepover, or inviting a friend to church are all forms of hospitality. Won't it be fun to find out we made an angel feel welcome?

I saw hospitality in action when ....

....

....

....

I could make someone else feel welcome by ....

....

....

....

God, guide me in ....

....

....

Today, I pray for ....

....

....

PRAISE AND REFLECT:
Gratitude

"Praise the Lord, my soul, and forget not all his benefits."
—Psalm 103:2

Gratitude is a becoming attribute in God's children. And
it's good for us, too! Before you go to bed, try focusing on
things that make you feel grateful. God will be pleased, and
you just might sleep better. Consider using the margins of
this page to doodle some things you are grateful for. Look
back over your journal for ideas. What might help you
remember to thank God for your blessings each day?

God, I am so grateful for ....

....

....

....

....

....

....

....

....

....

....

Love

Love is patient, love is kind. It does not envy,
it does not boast, it is not proud.

—1 Corinthians 13:4

You might have heard this Scripture read at a wedding, but it's not actually about romance. These words tell us how to love anyone God puts in our path. Real love puts the other person's feelings first, and it isn't filled with drama. Is there someone in your life who loves you like that?

Someone who has loved me well is ....

....

....

....

Someone I think I have loved well is ....

....

....

....

God, guide me in ....

....

....

Today, I pray for ....

....

....

Shame

Anyone who believes in [Jesus] will never be put to shame.
—Romans 10:11

Guilt is the feeling that you've *done* something wrong. Shame is the feeling that there's *something wrong with you.* Shame arrived with Adam and Eve's sin in the Garden of Eden, and it's been passed along to every person ever since. But Jesus died to make us new. With Him, we're no longer stuck in shame. God is making us beautiful, and that's how He already sees us!

To me, shame feels like ....

....

....

....

I don't have to be ashamed because ....

....

....

....

God, guide me in ....

....

....

....

Today, I pray for ....

....

....

86

Truth

Buy the truth and do not sell it—wisdom,
instruction and insight as well.
—Proverbs 23:23

There are different kinds of truth. The facts we learn in science or
the truth behind an upsetting conflict represent one kind. The truth
of our own feelings and experiences is another kind. Then there are
spiritual truths, like the depths of God's love, which we can only learn
in God's Word. All precious truths come from God.

A recent important truth I learned is ....

....

....

....

It can be hard to know what's true when ....

....

....

....

God, guide me in ....

....

....

Today, I pray for ....

....

....

Your Changing Body

I praise you because I am fearfully and wonderfully made;
your works are wonderful, I know that full well.
—Psalm 139:14

God doesn't make mistakes, but there are days when it might seem that way. While your body is growing into adulthood, it can go through some weird, uncomfortable changes. Like a caterpillar in a chrysalis, you're on your way to something new. And God says it's going to be wonderful!

A change I have noticed in my body is ....

....

....

I hope my body will one day be ....

....

....

God, guide me in ....

....

....

Today, I pray for ....

....

....

Gossip

In the same way, the women are to be worthy of respect, not malicious talkers but temperate and trustworthy in everything.
—1 Timothy 3:11

It's not wrong to talk about someone when they aren't around—if we are speaking well of them. But when we say negative things we wouldn't say to a person's face, that's gossip. Even online. Even if it's true. Gossiping makes it hard for people to trust us, and it hurts God's heart. But every day is a new chance to make a positive change.

Someone who needs healing from the hurt of gossip is ....

....

....

I am sorry for participating in gossip when ....

....

....

God, guide me in ....

....

....

Today, I pray for ....

....

....

Teamwork

[T]he whole body, joined and held together by every supporting
ligament, grows and builds itself up in love, as each part does its work.
—Ephesians 4:16

This Bible verse is talking about people working together to make
good things happen. Just as the foot has a separate, important
purpose from the hand, different people have different gifts and purposes. Whether your family is cleaning the attic or your whole town is
building a park, God has given you an important part to play.

A team I worked well with was ....

....

....

I am an important part of these groups: ....

....

....

God, guide me in ....

....

....

Today, I pray for ....

....

....

Second Chances

I write this to you so that you will not sin. But if anybody does sin, we have an advocate with the Father—Jesus Christ, the Righteous One.

—1 John 2:1

When we sin, as we all do, is there a limit to the number of times God will forgive us? No, because there's no limit to Jesus's willingness to step in for us. As long as our hearts are truly repentant, God will continue to forgive us every time. That's how big His love is.

When I worry about God's forgiveness, I can remember ....

....

....

....

Something I've been forgiven for is ....

....

....

....

God, guide me in ....

....

....

Today, I pray for ....

....

....

Parents

*Listen to your father, who gave you life, and do
not despise your mother when she is old.*
—Proverbs 23:22

If you have a child someday, you'll want them to pay attention to you
and be grateful for your love and care. The people God chose to raise
you to adulthood are making a huge investment in your life. We don't
often think about it, but that really deserves our appreciation.

The adults in my life are investing in me by ....

....

....

....

One way I could show appreciation would be ....

....

....

God, guide me in ....

....

....

Today, I pray for ....

....

....

Worry

Can any one of you by worrying add a single hour to your life?
—Matthew 6:27

There are two kinds of worry: productive and unproductive. Productive worry leads to constructive actions, like studying for a test or making a reminder list. But unproductive worry concerns something you can't change, like the weather or other people's decisions. Letting unproductive worry take up brain space isn't helping you. Try saying "No!" to that kind of worry.

I mostly worry about ....

....

....

....

When I'm worried about something I can't change, I want to ......

....

....

....

God, guide me in ....

....

....

Today, I pray for ....

....

....

Boundaries

One who has unreliable friends soon comes to ruin, but there is a friend who sticks closer than a brother.

—Proverbs 18:24

How can you tell when a relationship might be unhealthy? One way is by looking at the amount of give and take. Can you rely on your friend when you have needs or is the relationship a one-way street? When it's all give and no take, that might be a sign you need to set a few healthy boundaries. All solid relationships have them.

For me, a healthy relationship looks like ....

....

....

I might need to set a few boundaries with ....

....

....

God, guide me in ....

....

....

Today, I pray for ....

....

....

Doing Your Best

*Whatever you do, work at it with all your
heart, as working for the Lord.*
—Colossians 3:23

The world seems to say the truest measure of our effort is the outcome, like making the team or getting an A. But God says doing our best for Him is the truest measure of our effort, no matter the outcome. When God looks at our lives, it's not the team jersey or the top grade He sees as important. It's the heart behind it all.

Although I didn't succeed, I put in my best effort at ....

....

....

....

When God looks at my life, I hope He sees ....

....

....

....

God, guide me in ....

....

....

....

Today, I pray for ....

....

....

Change

*So do not fear, for I am with you; do not be dismayed, for
I am your God. I will strengthen you and help you.*

—Isaiah 41:10

All changes are stressful. There are hard ones like losing a friend and
good ones like graduating. When your emotional energy gets zapped
by life's changes, you could start to feel irritable, worried, or weepy.
Fortunately, God can give you new strength. Spend some time telling
Him about the changes you're going through. Try asking Him for help.

Some changes in my life recently are ....

....

....

When changes stress me out, I usually feel ....

....

....

God, guide me in ....

....

....

Today, I pray for ....

....

....

96

Motives

[The Lord] will bring to light what is hidden in darkness and will expose the motives of the heart.
—1 Corinthians 4:5

Only God knows what other people are thinking. Motives can be hidden, even from ourselves. Maybe we're slamming cupboards because we don't like dinner, or maybe we're upset about something our friend said earlier. It's probably best to question our own motives and assume good things about others' hearts.

Someone misjudged my heart when ....

....

....

I may have misjudged someone else's heart when ....

....

....

God, guide me in ....

....

....

Today, I pray for ....

....

....

PRAISE AND REFLECT:
Spiritual Growth

We may stop growing physically, but we never stop growing spiritually. God peels away the layers of our hearts like an onion, exposing what He wants to heal or teach us next. Praying and journaling each day is a great way to take the next step in this lifelong journey called "spiritual growth."

Since starting your journal, what is one thing you've learned?

Is there an area where you would like to
ask God for help or healing?

Is there an area you think God is highlighting
right now for your growth?

God, I praise you for working in me ....

....

....

....

....

....

....

....

....

Peace With God

Therefore, since we have been justified through faith, we have peace with God through our Lord Jesus Christ.

—Romans 5:1

You may have noticed most of the world is involved in an invisible war against the God of the universe. By not putting Him at the center of our lives, something else is our god. But when we believe in Jesus, and tell God how much we love Him, the war is over. His love is ours forever. We have peace with God.

To me, peace with God means ....

....

....

....

I am thankful for peace with God because ....

....

....

....

God, guide me in ....

....

....

Today, I pray for ....

....

....

Finding Your Voice

*[S]peaking the truth in love, we will grow to become
in every respect the mature body of . . . Christ.*
—Ephesians 4:15

God wants each of us to find our voice, to speak *our* truth into *our*
world. When we do that, God is revealed through us in unique ways,
in our own style, to our own people. These are the only rules: tell the
truth and always speak with loving motives.

I think I used my voice well when I ....

....

....

....

An area where I might be able to use my voice more is ....

....

....

....

God, guide me in ....

....

....

Today, I pray for ....

....

....

The Poor

Whoever is kind to the poor lends to the Lord, and he will reward them for what they have done.
—Proverbs 19:17

God has a big heart for the poor and the vulnerable. We are His hands and feet, to go to the less fortunate and help them. That might mean traveling to another country or maybe just walking around the corner. It could be supporting a cause online. Having a generous heart means you are becoming more like Jesus.

Someone I know who helps the poor is ....

....

....

....

Maybe I could help the poor by ....

....

....

....

God, guide me in ....

....

....

....

Today, I pray for ....

....

....

....

Pain

See, I have refined you, though not as silver; I have tested you in the furnace of affliction.

—Isaiah 48:10

No one wants to go through physical or emotional pain. The Bible tells us that when we go through hard things, God is with us, helping us. And, if we are willing, He will use our pain to make us holy, just as fire purifies silver and gold.

If I have to go through pain, I hope God will ....

....

....

....

The deepest pain I've been through is ....

....

....

God, guide me in ....

....

....

Today, I pray for ....

....

....

Romance

For your Maker is your husband—the
Lord Almighty is his name.
—Isaiah 54:5

It's fun to think about having a special person in your life. Or maybe you already have one. God wants us to have relationships, but He wants to remain the most important person in our heart, too. We have plenty of room for both.

I want the special person in my life to be ....

....

....

....

I could keep God first in my love life by ....

....

....

....

God, guide me in ....

....

....

....

Today, I pray for ....

....

....

Patience

... being strengthened with all power according to his glorious might so that you may have great endurance and patience.

—Colossians 1:11

Paul prayed this prayer for some new Christians who were experiencing hardships. It's hard to wait for an answer when you're struggling. We need patience for our own problems and for walking with friends and family who have troubles, too. God has infinite patience to give us, and He's available whenever we call.

God gave me patience when ....

....

....

....

Right now I need patience for ....

....

....

....

God, guide me in ....

....

....

....

Today, I pray for ....

....

....

In God's Image

*[T]here before me was a great multitude ... from
every nation, tribe, people and language, standing
before the throne and before the Lamb.*

—Revelation 7:9

Are adults better than kids? Are athletes better than nerds? No and
no. All people have equal dignity and value because they are made in
God's image. Every type of person will be standing together with us in
Heaven eventually. Why not learn to love them all now?

Sometimes people think they are better than ....

....

....

....

I like being with different kinds of people because ....

....

....

....

God, guide me in ....

....

....

Today, I pray for ....

....

....

Money

*No one can serve two masters . . . [Y]ou will be devoted to the one
and despise the other. You cannot serve both God and money.*
—Matthew 6:24

Have you ever thought about how we spend money? God says it
reveals a piece of our hearts. Some of us have the tendency to spend
money easily without thinking about the future. Some of us might
forget to be generous. Because our money is given to us by God, it's
always a good idea to ask Him about it.

I sometimes struggle with money when ....

....

....

I think a person who is wise about money ....

....

....

God, guide me in ....

....

....

Today, I pray for ....

....

....

Forgiving Others

For if you forgive other people when they sin against you, your heavenly Father will also forgive you.

—Matthew 6:14

Forgiving those who hurt us isn't optional. But it *can* be a process that takes time and prayer. Forgiveness means giving up the right to punish somebody, knowing God will be in charge of any consequences they need, now or in eternity. Our job is to give Him that job—and not take it back again.

I would like to forgive ....

....

....

....

When I forgive someone, I usually feel ....

....

....

....

God, guide me in ....

....

....

....

Today, I pray for ....

....

....

Growing Up

Then our sons in their youth will be like well-nurtured plants, and our daughters will be like pillars carved to adorn a palace.
—Psalm 144:12

The Bible describes maturity as *fruitfulness* and *strength*. Plants grow by weathering storms and digging deep. A house is built by cutting down trees and hammering nails. Growing up isn't always easy, but it prepares us for things we can't yet see. God is getting us ready to be beautiful and productive for His Kingdom.

A hard thing that helped me grow was ....

....

....

....

When I'm an adult, I hope I can ....

....

....

....

God, guide me in ....

....

....

....

Today, I pray for ....

....

....

Social Media

*The Lord does not look at the things people look at. People look
at the outward appearance, but the Lord looks at the heart.*
—1 Samuel 16:7

It's important to know social media doesn't always tell the whole
truth. Everyone lives their best life online. No one posts about being
stood up, flunking a test, or their latest makeup fail. Just as our outward appearance should be an honest reflection of a beautiful heart,
so should our social media.

Social media makes me feel ....

....

....

....

When I post on social media, I want to ....

....

....

....

God, guide me in ....

....

....

Today, I pray for ....

....

....

Listening

To answer before listening—that is folly and shame.
—Proverbs 18:13

Think about somebody who really listens to you. That's somebody who really cares about you. Those who don't listen to you miss what's in your heart. God always cares and is never too busy to listen. He can help us slow down and hear the hearts around us, too.

A good listener in my life is ....

....

....

....

When someone really listens to me, I feel ....

....

....

....

God, guide me in ....

....

....

....

Today, I pray for ....

....

....

....

Why

*"Rabbi, who sinned, this man or his
parents, that he was born blind?"*

*"Neither this man nor his parents sinned," said Jesus, "but this
happened so that the works of God might be displayed in him."*

—John 9:2-3

When bad things happen, we want to know why. While God might not explain it all to us, His mercy and power do shine through the difficult times. When bad things happen, look for all the ways God shows up.

I saw God show up in a bad situation when ....

....

....

....

A question I have about my life is ....

....

....

....

God, guide me in ....

....

....

Today, I pray for ....

....

....

PRAISE AND REFLECT:
Beauty

"For the beauty of the earth, for the beauty of the skies . . ." So begins a famous hymn of praise by Folliott Sandford Pierpoint. Beauty is a special gift God created to connect our hearts to His. He shows us all this beauty so it's easier to imagine how very beautiful *He* must be.

What is something beautiful that makes your heart soar? Is there anything beautiful in your room? Pictures, fabric, art? List a few ways you find beauty in other people. Look back over your journal for ideas.

I praise you, Lord, for the beauty I see in ....

....

....

....

....

....

....

....

....

....

....

....

Grace

*But to each one of us grace has been given
as Christ apportioned it.*

—Ephesians 4:7

Grace means God's favor and His divine influence on our hearts.
Grace isn't something we earn or deserve. It is the gift of faith and
all that faith does *in us*. Grace is like a pipeline pouring God's love
out toward others. Grace changes us, and through us it can change
the world.

To me, grace means ....

....

....

....

A gift of grace I can give the world is ....

....

....

....

God, guide me in ....

....

....

Today, I pray for ....

....

....

Witnessing

Jesus ... said, "Go home to your own people and tell them how much the Lord has done for you, and how he has had mercy on you."
—Mark 5:19

Anyone with the Holy Spirit living inside them is a "witness" for God. You can talk about your own experiences and about how God has worked in your life. Witnessing for Jesus doesn't have to be a presentation you memorize, although that's fine, too. It can just be you, loving people and letting them know you are a Christian.

A time I was a witness for God was ....

....

....

....

If someone asked me about Jesus, I could say ....

....

....

....

God, guide me in ....

....

....

....

Today, I pray for ....

....

....

Making Peace

*Blessed are the peacemakers, for they
will be called children of God.*

—Matthew 5:9

Jesus came to earth to bring us the peace of God. When we make peace in the world around us, we're doing His work, too. Sometimes all it takes is ignoring unimportant irritations, being a gracious loser, or putting our own needs off for a little while. That's a small price to pay for peace.

I made peace when ....

....

....

....

Being a peacemaker makes me feel ....

....

....

....

God, guide me in ....

....

....

....

Today, I pray for ....

....

....

Spiritual Warfare

*Put on the full armor of God, so that you can take
your stand against the devil's schemes.*
—Ephesians 6:11

The Christian life can be a struggle. Our enemy, Satan, wants us to
fail in our fight to be faithful. He'll use all kinds of lies to trick us into
doubt or sin. But God has given us weapons like faith, the Holy Spirit,
Scripture, prayer, and our spiritual community. When you sense a
battle coming, grab your weapons and fight the good fight!

A spiritual battle I fought recently was ....

....

....

....

The spiritual weapons I use most are ....

....

....

....

God, guide me in ....

....

....

Today, I pray for ....

....

....

Exercise

After all, no one ever hated their own body, but they feed and care for their body, just as Christ does the church.
—Ephesians 5:29

Your body needs your help. It needs you to practice regular healthy habits of nutrition, sleep, and exercise. Staying active will help you feel better, physically and emotionally. If you don't have an exercise plan, why not ask God (and maybe a friend) to help you make one?

I take good care of my body by ....

....

....

....

In terms of exercise, I would like to ....

....

....

God, guide me in ....

....

....

Today, I pray for ....

....

....

Fellowship

They devoted themselves to the apostles' teaching and to fellowship, to the breaking of bread and to prayer.

—Acts 2:42

Churches today teach God's Word, share communion, pray, and hang out together because this is what the early Church did. While those first Christians may not have been playing volleyball or watching movies, they were doing life and ministry together and, yes, having fun. Aren't you glad God wants His children to live that way?

I'm glad God wants us to have fellowship because ....

....

....

....

An example of Christian fellowship in my life is ....

....

....

....

God, guide me in ....

....

....

Today, I pray for ....

....

....

Anger

*In your anger do not sin: Do not let the sun
go down while you are still angry.*

—Ephesians 4:26

Jesus got angry, so feeling anger can't be sinful; it's what we *do* with
our anger that matters. God can use anger to motivate us to right
wrongs or defend the weak. But when there's nothing we can do, it's
tempting to lash out. Try going for a run or journaling instead. By
using your anger productively, you'll feel better.

I feel angry when ....

....

....

....

Something I could try next time I feel angry is ....

....

....

....

God, guide me in ....

....

....

Today, I pray for ....

....

....

Choices

Who, then, are those who fear the Lord? He will
instruct them in the ways they should choose.

—Psalm 25:12

Some people think God doesn't care about small choices. But small choices can have big consequences. If you go to the party Friday night, you might meet a new friend. But that lost study time might have helped you ace biology. It's appropriate to consult the Lord in all our choices, big and small, because only He knows the outcome.

A small choice that had big consequences was ....

....

....

....

The next small choice I have to make is ....

....

....

....

God, guide me in ....

....

....

....

Today, I pray for ....

....

....

Moving Forward

Forgetting what is behind and straining toward what is ahead,
I press on toward . . . the prize for which God has called me.
—Philippians 3:13–14

Sometimes the past drags us back toward guilt or regret. Or it can haunt us with memories of a better time. We can deal with the past by capturing it in writing, praying through it, and offering forgiveness or gratitude. Then it's time to move forward, putting the past in the past. God has new possibilities ahead.

Something I often think about is ....

....

....

....

Sometimes the past keeps me from ....

....

....

....

God, guide me in ....

....

....

....

Today, I pray for ....

....

....

....

Stress

The seed falling among the thorns refers to someone who hears the word, but the worries of this life ... [make] it unfruitful.
—Matthew 13:22

A small rock held close to your eyes will block the view of everything else. Our problems can do that, too. It's important to look at bigger things, like the faithfulness of God and our life past this present stress. Imagine yourself a week *after* your problem is over. Focusing beyond our troubles helps make them smaller.

A problem stressing me out right now is ....

....

....

....

Something bigger I could focus on would be ....

....

....

....

God, guide me in ....

....

....

....

Today, I pray for ....

....

....

Relationships

Do to others as you would have them do to you.

—Luke 6:31

So much of what God has to say about relationships comes down to the Golden Rule from Luke 6. Whether we're thinking about our best friend, someone we dislike, or a stranger on the street, God asks us to treat them the way we would want to be treated: with courtesy, patience, and kindness. That's relationship gold.

I want to follow the Golden Rule with people I dislike by ....

....

....

....

A time when a stranger treated me well was ....

....

....

....

God, guide me in ....

....

....

Today, I pray for ....

....

....

Empowerment

He gives strength to the weary and
increases the power of the weak.

—Isaiah 40:29

We often feel powerless to change things. When you're a teen, other people, like parents and teachers, make a lot of the decisions for you. But you *do* have the power of conversation and the power of prayer. Since God is the source of infinite power, He can empower you to make a difference. You just have to ask!

I feel powerless to ....

....

....

....

I need God's power to help me ....

....

....

....

God, guide me in ....

....

....

....

Today, I pray for ....

....

....

Character

[T]he fruit of the Spirit is love, joy, peace, forbearance, kindness, goodness, faithfulness, gentleness and self-control.

—Galatians 5:22–23

Everybody knows it's important to develop strong character, but what does that actually mean? God gives us this little summary as a starting place. Notice some of these qualities grow best in times of hardship. No one wants problems, but tackling difficulties is one way we get the character we *do* want.

My best friend would describe my character as ....

....

....

....

A quality I've seen grow in hard times is ....

....

....

....

God, guide me in ....

....

....

....

Today, I pray for ....

....

....

PRAISE AND REFLECT:
Benediction

A benediction, or blessing, is a special kind of prayer spoken over people starting or concluding something. You can bless someone who's leaving for school, going to bed, or starting a new job. As you finish your prayer journal, may you feel God's blessing!

Who could you pray a blessing over today?
(It doesn't have to be out loud.)

Focus on God's affection for you as you read this benediction: "May the grace of the Lord Jesus Christ, and the love of God, and the fellowship of the Holy Spirit be with you." (2 Corinthians 13:14)

Thank you, Lord, for blessing me with ....
....
....
....
....
....
....
....
....
....

Temptation

God is faithful; he will not let you be tempted beyond what you can bear . . . He will also provide a way out so that you can endure it.
—1 Corinthians 10:13

It's not a sin to have tempting thoughts. Jesus was also tempted. But when we begin to play with those thoughts, imagining how it would feel to give in, that's where trouble starts. When you feel tempted, try praying about it. Distract yourself with good things. Then watch for the way of escape God provides.

A temptation I've faced is ....

....

....

....

God gave me a way out of temptation when ....

....

....

....

God, guide me in ....

....

....

Today, I pray for ....

....

....

Time

*A thousand years in your sight are like a day that
has just gone by, or like a watch in the night.*

—Psalm 90:4

When you were four, a week seemed like forever. Now maybe a year
seems unbearably long. As we get older, time passes with greater and
greater speed. That's important to remember as we are going through
trials or waiting for something we want. What seems like an eternity
now is only a moment to God—and it *will* pass.

Right now, I wish time would

Time seemed really long when

God, guide me in

Today, I pray for

Commitment

Let us hold unswervingly to the hope we profess,
for he who promised is faithful.
—Hebrews 10:23

Life can be like riding a bike down a gravel road. Even the greatest Christians who've ever lived had days when doubt or temptation or pain made them lose their balance. It's our part to encourage ourselves to hope, to try our best, and to pray. It's God's part to help us keep our commitment to Him.

A commitment I've kept is ....

....

....

I find it hard sometimes to stay committed to my faith when ......

....

....

....

God, guide me in ....

....

....

Today, I pray for ....

....

....

Self-Image

Your beauty should not come from outward adornment . . . it should be that of your inner self.

—1 Peter 3:3–4

Most of us don't want to be judged on our appearance, though we worry about it. We want to be judged by our hearts. That's where our self-image should come from, too. Maybe you could paste some sticky notes on your mirror listing positive inner qualities you have. That might help you see the things God sees.

My self-image is ....

....

....

....

Some of my thoughts about me I'd like to change are ....

....

....

....

God, guide me in ....

....

....

....

Today, I pray for ....

....

....

Accountability

Plans fail for lack of counsel, but with many advisers they succeed.

—Proverbs 15:22

It can be really upsetting when we make a big mistake. But we're all fallible, and we all fall into traps we don't see. We need wise guides who can lovingly help us face and grow from our mistakes. This might be someone older or just someone trustworthy we can open up to. Do you have someone like that in your life?

I might be able to open up my life to ....

....

....

....

Maybe I could provide accountability for someone else like ....

....

....

....

God, guide me in ....

....

....

Today, I pray for ....

....

....

Service

Each of you should use whatever gift you have received to serve others, as faithful stewards of God's grace in its various forms.

—1 Peter 4:10

Are you good at language, organization, hospitality, sports, or music? God has given everybody their own gifts. But God didn't bless you with those abilities just for you. He gave you your gifts so you can bless others, and an amazing result of serving people is that it usually makes us feel good, too!

I think a way I could serve others is ....

....

....

....

Serving others makes me feel ....

....

....

....

God, guide me in ....

....

....

....

Today, I pray for ....

....

....

....

Disappointment

For our light and momentary troubles are achieving for us an eternal glory that far outweighs them all.

—2 Corinthians 4:17

When things don't work out the way we hoped, it's natural to be disappointed. And while God wants to comfort us in those moments, He also wants us to look beyond our present circumstances. When we rely on God despite our sadness or frustration, we're storing up glory in Heaven.

A recent disappointment for me was ....

....

....

....

One way I relied on God when I was disappointed was ....

....

....

....

God, guide me in ....

....

....

....

Today, I pray for ....

....

....

Work

May the favor of the Lord our God rest on us; establish the work of our hands for us—yes, establish the work of our hands.

—Psalm 90:17

So much that we call work doesn't feel very important, like doing homework, making our bed, or babysitting. It's all just going to be repeated. And yet, our labor is a piece of us we put out into the world, something we can do to help others in our own special way, and something God cares about. That makes it important.

Work I need to do soon is ....

....

....

....

God could help me with that work by ....

....

....

....

God, guide me in ....

....

....

Today, I pray for ....

....

....

Joy

...for the joy of the Lord is your strength.

—Nehemiah 8:10

Joy isn't the same thing as happiness. Joy is a spiritual connection to God we can sense in all kinds of circumstances. We can even experience joy in the midst of hardship or pain. When you feel a tingle saying God is pleased because you shared your lunch, that's joy. When a glow in your heart tells you God will take care of you despite missing the bus, that's joy. And those small joys can give us strength.

I felt joy when ....

....

....

....

Joy gives me strength because ....

....

....

....

God, guide me in ....

....

....

Today, I pray for ....

....

....

Confession

Therefore confess your sins to each other and pray for each other so that you may be healed.

—James 5:16

While we can and should confess our sins to God, we can also talk with a person close to us. When we do, their prayers and their love can help us heal. The next time you're walking around with a heavy load of guilt, try confessing to someone you really trust. You might just feel a whole lot better.

Today, I need to confess ....

....

....

....

I think someone safe I could talk to might be ....

....

....

....

God, guide me in ....

....

....

Today, I pray for ....

....

....

Obedience

And may your hearts be fully committed to the Lord our God, to live by his decrees and obey his commands.

—1 Kings 8:61

Wise King Solomon prayed this prayer over his people because it's a *blessing* to obey God. The Lord doesn't give us laws to be mean. God gave us the Commandments to stay safe, become wise, do good, and love others well. Obedience is a blessing—to us and to the world.

I was obedient to God when ....

....

....

I think it's wise to obey God because ....

....

....

God, guide me in ....

....

....

Today, I pray for ....

....

....

Leadership

Since an overseer manages God's household, he must be ... hospitable, one who loves what is good, who is self-controlled, upright, holy and disciplined.

—Titus 1:7–8

Who is a leader you admire? What are their best qualities? God says His leaders must look to their own hearts before they guide others and have a reputation for warmth, patience, and integrity. The best leaders are also the best followers—Jesus's followers.

Qualities of a good leader are ....

....

....

....

An opportunity I have to lead is ....

....

....

God, guide me in ....

....

....

Today, I pray for ....

....

....

Wisdom

*So give your servant a discerning heart to govern your
people and to distinguish between right and wrong.*
—1 Kings 3:9

King Solomon could have wished for riches, land, or power, but he
asked God for wisdom instead. Wisdom, or discernment, means
knowing how to make the best choices. Most people get wisdom
by learning from their mistakes, but we can also read God's Word,
observe the world, and ask God for wisdom, like Solomon did.

Something wise I did was ....

....

....

....

I would like more wisdom in the area of ....

....

....

....

God, guide me in ....

....

....

....

Today, I pray for ....

....

....

Final Reflections

Wow! You've finished your whole journal—a part of your own story you've written with God. Spend a little time reflecting on what you've learned and what the next chapter might look like.

Writing out my thoughts has been ....

....

....

....

....

....

Some things I've learned about myself are ....

....

....

....

....

....

Some things I've learned about others are ....

....

....

....

....

Some things I've learned about God are ....

....

....

....

....

....

Journaling my prayers has changed my relationship with

God by ....

....

....

....

....

....

Now that I've finished this journal, I'd like to ....

....

....

....

....

....

Index of Topics

Scripture Index

About the Author

 **Louise Holzhauer** is an experienced counselor, wife, and mother of two grown children. She lives in Florida with her husband, Greg, and her dog, Maggie. She has a couple of master's degrees from Reformed Theological Seminary, and she is a licensed therapist. Perhaps her most important credential is surviving a life-and-death battle with cancer at the age of 21. That journey taught her a lot about dark days, painful problems, and God's love.

Louise enjoys leading small groups, writing devotionals, spending the summer months in Michigan, reading nonfiction, and babysitting her three amazing grandchildren—sometimes all at once. She writes a lot of things, and you can read some of them on her website at DearChristianCounselor.com.